Body Language For Beginners

Learn To Recognize Non-Verbal Signs

Brian Hall

Body Language For Beginners

TABLE OF CONTENTS

INTRODUCTION 6

CHAPTER 1 WHO SHOULD KNOW BODY LANGUAGE AND WHY...8

CHAPTER 2 FIRST IMPRESSIONS 16

HANDSHAKE 18

BODY ORIENTATION 24

HOW THEY WALK 28

HEAD... 38

ARMS.. 43

LEGS 56

CHAPTER 3: NON-VERBAL LANGUAGE   HOW THE BRAIN CONTROLS BODY LANGUAGE 62

CHAPTER 4   NON VERBAL SIGNALS 66

THE LOWER BODY 68

THE UPPER BODY... 70

THE HANDS... 72

THE FACE 76

SIGNS OF NEGATIVE EMOTIONS........................ 78

SIGNS OF POSITIVE EMOTIONS......................... 86

UNIVERSAL NON-VERBAL SIGNALS.................... 90

CHAPTER 5   THE SECRET IS IN THE BREATH.........................98

CONCLUSION 102

Introduction

Do you know what it means to read body language?

It's okay if you don't. Not many people do. It's a subtle art that can let you in on things about another person and how they feel about you. Knowing how to read a person's body language can give you so many insights into the people around you.

While it may sound fancy, reading body language means that you pay attention to how other's move, use their hands, and their tone of voice. Something that may seem as insignificant as touching their face can speak volumes when you know how to read body language.

Reading body language is famously used by the FBI, and other types of agencies, to help them find perpetrators. They know how to spot a liar from a mile away. While it's likely not a normal part of the training, this would be a good skill for cops and lawyers as well.

While there are a lot of careers that can benefit from this skill, reading body language can be helpful in everyday life. You will no longer have to wonder if your friends sincerely care about you, or if your significant other loves you.

This book will take you through the basics of body language from first impressions to micro expressions. You will know what to look for and what each little movement means.

We will even go into how the brain affects these movements people make. Body language is pretty much a subconscious act. Nobody realizes what they are doing, and that's what makes reading it such a powerful tool. People can use a fake smile, but the way they use their body will allow you to see past the smile. Understanding the way that the brain controls all of this will also help you to understand further how powerful body language is.

Let's get started.

Chapter 1

Who Should Know Body Language and Why

B ody language is a very important part of communication that only a few people study, yet it takes up most of how we communicate and is normally more accurate than the meaning of words.

You've heard that actions speak louder than words, and this couldn't be truer because there are some things you can communicate without saying a word. A shrug of the shoulders can tell somebody, "I don't know." A raise of the eyebrows can say, "Did I hear that right?" Having your palms turned up and shrug a bit, it says, "I don't know what else to do." Pointing to your nose can mean, "That's right."

The way we use our bodies helps to reinforce the things we say. You can simply say, "I don't know," or you can add this gesture; turn your palms face up in front of you, raise your eyebrows, frown a little, and stick out your bottom lip. At this point, you have also made somebody laugh and taken some pressure off yourself or anybody who was nervous.

Why do people bother with the imprecise and hard work of trying to figure out body language? I mean, we are an expert at it already with the unconscious mind, and our unconscious mind is already better, faster, and immensely more powerful than our conscious minds. Why should we take the time and do the hard work of moving out unconscious expertise to our conscious mind, make it worse, struggling with improving it, before pushing it back down into our unconscious mind once we stop focusing on it in our awake brain?

The reason we should do all of this work is that it allows us to develop the skill of reading the body language of others, and how to control our own. Learning this skill will allow us to become better communicators that use intent instead of leaving communication up to chance.

For example, when we meet a person for the very first time, our unconscious mind starts trying to develop answers to certain questions that evolution has taught us are important. Are they a friend or an enemy? Are they more or less powerful than I am? Are they a potential mate? Do they understand what they are saying? And then as the relationship deepens, the big question is, can I trust them?

By communicating with intent, can you use body language to create some form of trust with another person more quickly and reliably than leaving it all to the unconscious mind? This is a question that salespeople are very interested in, but this is true for speakers as well, since an audience wants to trust the person on stage, and the answer to this question is going to determine if they buy into whatever you are trying to tell them.

A great way to improve the likelihood and speed of trust building is to mirror what the other person does. This is a very well-studied phenomenon in the body language world. You can look around and see co-workers, friends, and lovers unconsciously mirroring each other and agree on things easily, which is our body's way of telling others, "Hey, we act alike, we agree on the same things, we are working on the same page."

A person can consciously mirror a complete stranger, which will greatly improve their rate and depth of trust-building. This should be done subtly and carefully, but it is pretty rare for a person to notice this happening unless you become extremely hyperactive in mirroring every single twitch they make.

But how does this help speakers? How could a speaker possibly mirror an audience? There are quite a few ways.

First, align yourself with them by moving into them and turn to face the stage like you were an audience member. Second, when you get the chance to interact with individual people, possibly during a Q and A, you can mirror that person. Thirdly, you can act out something and then have the audience participate. Just make sure it is relevant. You are only going to cause more questions if you start making everybody do jumping jacks for no reason.

The conscious study and use of body language for psychological purposes is hard work, but what you get in return is being about to make stronger connections with those around.

Furthermore, through reading body language, you can spot when a person starts to lie. There is a chapter later on that covers how to spot a liar, but the most common sign of a lie is not being able to keep eye contact because they believe their eyes are going to give away their little secret. However, there are some not so common signs of lying.

Some people like to clear their throat, change the pitch of their voice, or stutter a lot when lying. They may try to pull your attention to something to distract you or stall the conversation to come up with a plausible explanation. Additionally, tapping their foot, bouncing, rubbing their face, blushing, looking away, or raising their shoulder could be an indicator that they aren't completely comfortable in the conversation because they aren't truthful. These are only a few examples, and we will go over more later on.

Something else that body language helps with is expressing our feelings. When you pay attention to nonverbal signs, it helps you to figure out how the person feels about the things they are saying. For example, somebody could agree to do something, but their body language tells you that they don't want to. This can be helpful if you are a manager or in a leadership position so that you can figure out who would be the best at an assignment. If somebody's heart isn't in it, then they probably won't do the best job.

When it comes to job interviews, body language is sometimes the determining factor. If the applicant conveys confidence and eases with the subject matter through their body language, they have a better chance of getting the job. As we have discussed, body language can cause somebody to seem out of control or uncomfortable. These types of traits cause a job applicant to come off as less comfortable and confident.

When you are having a conversation with a person, their body language can let you know if they are paying attention to what you say or if they could care less. When they lean forward, they are saying they are interested. Leaning back could mean that they feel superior or aren't interested.

If a person is standing close to another and leaning forward while they talk, they could be trying to persuade the other person or dominate the conversation. If somebody is talking and you don't make eye contact, then you look like you aren't listening and just waiting to get to talk. This makes you seem like you don't care, and they may be less likely to listen to you when you do talk.

There is some body language that is easier to spot than other types. You will learn more about how to spot them throughout this book.

Albert Mehrabian

During the late 60s, Albert Mehrabian performed several experiments to learn how important intonation and gestures are for sharing a certain message. He discovered that only around seven percent of our communication is verbal. 39 percent of our communication is considered to be paraverbal, meaning intonation and tone, and then 55 percent of our communication is nonverbal. These percentages tell us that the movement of the body, hand movements, and simple gestures are an extremely important part of how humans communicate.

Now, these results are probably debatable because Mehrabian said that the results came from a controlled experiment, and they may not reflect a realistic setting. But it did give Mehrabian a chance to show that words alone do not give enough information to help a person completely understand your message.

- Intonation

Intonation is simply the varying pitch of the voice as you speak. Take the word "thanks," for example. This word is typically viewed as a positive word. However, if a person said "thanks" in a curt or firm tone, how would you feel? You are likely going to interpret it in a very different way, and it isn't going to come off as positive. Intonation plays a big part when it comes to conveying the feeling.

Intonation and facial expressions aren't all that different between cultures. Disgust, no matter where you are in the world, is going to be pretty easy to read. Similarly, intonations for sadness and happiness are typically easy to figure out no matter what part of the world you are in.

- Movements and Gestures

People often use gestures to convey the subtle bits of their messages. Gestures can even be used in place of words. For example, if you want a person to continue telling you about something interesting, you aren't likely to cut them off with "That's so cool! Can you tell me more?" You are probably going to lean forward to let them know that you are interested in learning more about what they are saying, or you could nod your head.

The majority of our gestures are with our hands. In the US, hello is often said by waving. Thumbs up is used to say something is good, or if we are really upset, we may use our middle finger. We can even show that we are impatient with our hands.

The Difficulties of Body Language

Brits and Americans have very familiar body language, and people of those countries find it easier to understand. There may be a few regional differences, but it still wouldn't be that hard to figure out. Now, for Americans or Brits, we would have probably understanding nonverbal communication from other cultures. While waving your hand means hello to us, in Croatia, it is seen as offensive. They think it looks too much like the Nazi salute.

Chapter 2
First Impressions

F irst impressions, as I'm sure you are aware, are an extremely important part of starting a relationship. First impressions are quickly made when meeting a person. For the most part, first impressions are made within 30 seconds of meeting somebody. The wrong body language can create a false impression because a person will read your body language before they listen to what you say.

In learning how to read body language, you can improve your first impressions as well as reading other people. First impressions are extremely dependent on nonverbal cues. Positive first impressions normally involve:

- Focusing on the other person.

- Appropriate eye contact.

- Eye contact shouldn't come off as an aggressive stare down.

- Don't look around the room like a maniac.

- Look where the focus of the conversation is.

- Standing tall with the chest centered and shoulders rolled back.

People who want to create a good relationship are going to make sure they are in an open posture. The inside of the palms should be shown regularly, which tells the other person, subconsciously, that they are welcomed and their message is important.

The trick is, for anybody looking to make a good impression; they also have to feel good on the inside. This has to be fulfilled if you want to show complete integrity on the outside.

We are going to go through the small things that you can look at when you first meet somebody. A person's slight movements, body position, and simple gestures can cue you into whether or not they are interested in what is said and much more. This information can then be used to ensure that a good first impression is made.

Handshake

Remember when you were first taught the "correct" way to shake hands? You want a firm, hard grip, right? Nobody wants to shake hands with a fish. It doesn't matter how successful you are; those few seconds that it takes to shake a person's hand will reveal more about them than any degree or title on a sheet of paper can.

Around the world, handshakes are recognized as a sign of hello. While a handshake may appear as a friendly gesture, it can also tell you something about that person's personality. This is what makes understanding the meanings of certain handshakes in different situations so important.

A handshake initiates a conversation is nearly any professional or social gathering. This introduction has the ability to make or break the feel of the environment.

A study published in the *Journal of Personality and Social Psychology* explained that people need to start paying attention to how other's shake hands. People are going to be making judgments and initial opinions based on a handshake.

The University of Alabama conducted a research study in 2000, where they tested 112 handshakes and compared the impressions they left with the paperwork they were asked to feel out.

They found that "firm handshake" was connected with personality traits like extroversion and being open to new things. Weak handshakes were connected to high levels of anxiety and shyness.

Women often have weaker handshakes then the men did, but women who hand firm handshakes received positive ratings. Even with women, strong handshakes meant a strong personality.

The different factors they had to use to judge the handshakes were quite complex. The "judges" of the handshakes were trained for a month and taught to look for eight characteristics:

- Eye contact
- Texture
- Vigor
- Duration
- Strength
- Dryness
- Temperature
- Completeness of grip

There are a lot of things to consider when all you are interested in is shaking hands to figure out the type of person they are. The easy part is that most of those characteristics correlated with each other, and this boils down to the judges looking at "weak impression," "positive impression," "weak," or "firm." The shakers who maintained eye contact, shook with Vigo and had warm, strong hands and grip, were viewed the most positively.

Chances are, if you have a firm handshake, you will have all of the other characteristics. Dr. William Chaplin, the study's lead, said that a person's handshake would stay the same throughout their life and stays in line with their personality. Body language experts are quite as positive.

They believe that even if you are introverted and shy, there are some things that you can do to show that you have strength behind your nerves.

Besides making sure you hold on and pull tight, you should also keep your body facing the other person to show that you are listening and open. When you shake hands while standing, it seems more positive, which is try for women and men, but you have to keep eye contact.

A person is seen as rude if they reach for a handshake when the other person clearly has their hands full. If you are at a party, you should keep your drinks in the left hand to keep your right dry and warm, ready for a handshake. This will also keep your hand warm and dry.

- Offering Handshakes

According to some cultural norms, a person is who of higher standing, like an elder or teacher, should be the one initiating the handshake instead of a person of lower standing. If you are about equal with the other person, when it comes to job and age, offering the handshake is a way to make yourself look confident, and you won't be surprised if the other person initiates one.

When you see world leaders shake hands, look for the person who appears the most relaxed and confident. A rule of thumb is, if you stand on the left in pictures, you will give off a better impression than standing on the right where you come off as submissive. You will also have the upper hand in the picture.

- Pressure

Making sure that you have the right amount of pressure during the shake plays just as big of a role as the shake. Men tend to squeeze harder, especially if you are trying to make a deal, show more confidence, or to provide a warm greeting.

The important thing about pressure is to have the appropriate squeeze for the situation. Being firm in your handshake, without crushing their hand, comes off as confident and is always better than a limp shake. Limp handshakes won't build rapport.

- The Noodle

A handshake that you can't even feel is exposing a weak inner-being. If this is used on an associate or employer, they are probably going to see this as low self-confidence and won't trust the person's skills.

Some think they have to be "gentle" when they shake a woman's hand, but they shouldn't. Female professionals respect and appreciate people who treat them like their male counterparts.

- The Crusher or Dominant Handshake

The complete opposite of the last handshake is the crusher. When a handshake is too powerful, it shows that they are trying to overcompensate for something. This will end up in people dismissing you.

- The Politician

This is where the initiator uses both hands to shake hands. The handshake is done like normal, but they also place their free hand on top.
This type of handshake is meant to show trust and honesty, not power. If they place the right hand on your elbow, they are saying that they really like you.

- Being Fancy

A lot of people have started to think they should make a handshake cooler. When they try to add something to a handshake, like a fist bump, they come off as immature and are completely unaware. This type of handshake, though, is perfectly okay amongst friends.

- The Lingerer

This is the person who likes to hold that handshake just a bit too long. Holding on too long makes them appear desperate. A handshake shouldn't last any longer than two seconds.

- The Rusher

While you don't want it too long, you also don't want it to be too short, which is the same as brushing off a person who is trying to tell you something. A short handshake shows their rude and that they don't care or have time for you. In some cases, it can also mean they are nervous.

- Looking Away

A good handshake doesn't just include the hands. A person should also make eye contact and smile. A person who lacks in this area shows that they may have some insecurity, suspiciousness, or shyness.

- The Stare Down

If you maintain really strong eye contact to the point where you are staring them down, this shows aggression, and even more so if the handshake lingers. Squinted eyes and pursed lips mean aggression.

- The Best Handshake

A perfect handshake is where the palms touch and the thumbs wrap around each other. The grasp is firm but not crushing, and the eye contact is soft and warm, showing that they are sincere and friendly.

Body Orientation

Let's take a moment to do a little visualization. Picture this, you are shopping, and you look around and see a friend from high school at the far end of the aisle, and you want to say hello. You walk back over to him. Yes, your back is turned towards him, just bear with me. As soon as you get closer to him, judging by the shadow he has cast on the floor, you say, "Hello Michael. What you been up to?"

You're going to freak him out. But this also shows the importance of body orientation when it comes to nonverbal communication. You could have stood there and talked to him with your back to him, but it just seemed nearly impossible to really communicate. We have all learned from an unwritten rule that you need to be in the "correct" position before you can start a conversation with a person.

The body naturally turns to whatever it wants.

You're probably thinking, "Yeah, and? Everybody already knows that. If you need something out of a cabinet, you turn to the cabinet. You want to watch television; you face the television." Sure, it is no big deal. But people tend to take an important piece of information for granted, and that this is true for humans.

We naturally turn toward the people that we want to engage with or pay attention to. The way our body is oriented reveals a lot about what or who we are interested in. When two people are having a conversation, you can learn a lot about how involved they are in the conversation by looking to see if they are parallel.

If two people, who are talking, face each other and place their shoulders parallel to each other, they have created a closed formation. This means that they are physically and psychologically rejecting everybody else so that they can focus on each other. You have probably intuitively spotted this, but think about what this means in a group setting and not just a two-person conversation. When you are watching a group of people talking, you can easily spot those who are more interested in one another by looking for the ones that standing parallel.

If you see a conversation of three, and two of them stand parallel to each other, then you can easily assume that the others are trying to push that third person out, or that third person has chosen to remove themselves from the conversation. There is also a chance that a third person would like to join a conversation but is currently a part of another group.

If you follow a straight line from that person, you will soon find the person that he is interested in and is trying to engage with. If you have two people talking, and they are clearly parallel, and a third tries to join, two things can happen at this moment. He will either be welcomed or rejected. How can you spot whether or not he will be welcomed or rejected by simply watching their body language?

- Welcomed

If they choose to welcome this new person in, they will have to change up their position to allow them in. At first, they are parallel and completely focused on one another, but now they have to welcome in a third, and they both have to give a bit of their attention to him.

They change up their position to redistribute their attention.

They will need to pivot to reach an angle of 45 degrees between both people to form a triable. The attention has now been divided amongst the group members.

When two people are 45 degrees to one another and not parallel, it might mean that they aren't completely into one another and are looking for a third person join them. It might mean that they both interested in this person. They would gladly accept that third person to join in a finish their triangle.

- Rejected

What happens if they want to reject the third person? When the third person steps up to these two, deep in conversation, they will look at him to answer what he has to say, but they won't open their body position to allow him to join in. This is a rejection, at least at that moment.

It might not mean that they hate him, but they don't want him to join in on their current conversation.

They are letting him know, nonverbally, "Please leave us along. We are talking." Most of the time, this person will take the hint and leave, or, if really desperate, will try to force his way in.

You can spot this in any group setting of any number, and not just three. The more people that are talking, the more circular that group will become so that everybody's attention is equally distributed. If people are distributing their attention equally, then you can assume that there are some outcasts.

- Some Caveats

Now, if you see people not parallel to each other, it doesn't necessarily mean that they aren't interested. If people are walking, or they are doing something that requires some type of physical activity, having a non-parallel body position doesn't always mean non-involvement.

People are also seen as aggressive if they walk straight up to another, so this is why people will walk up to you from a 45-degree angle to appear more positive and have a better chance of being welcomed into the conversation. To figure out for certain that people involved in a non-parallel conversation aren't interested in each other, you have to look at other things. For example, if they aren't talking that much and are looking around the room a lot, then they aren't into one another.

How They Walk

Let's say you are at a bar, and a person walks in like John Wayne. You could assume that he is tough and confident. Then again, you could have some other less polite thoughts. No matter how you view him, you find it hard to jump to conclusions based on the way he walks.

During the last three-quarters of the century, psychologies have had a look at these assumptions, and they discovered that everybody makes assumptions based on the way a person walks. After you watch the wannabe cowboy walk in, chances are, both of us are going to agree about his personality. But is this an accurate assumption? What types of characteristics can you read from a person's gait?

It might not be what you want to hear, but one of the best people to ask about walking and assumptions is a psychopath. Let's look at the research on the connection between personality and gait.

The earliest investigation into this was performed by Werner Wolf, a German-born psychologist, and published in 1935. He took eight people and recorded them walking while playing a ring-throwing game while wearing overalls. The overalls were to conceal any other personality giveaways.

Later, he had the participants watch the films, which he edited so that they couldn't see their heads. They all made their interpretations of one another's personalities based on how they walked.

There are some interesting little details about this study. For example, they had to use a metronome to mask the recordings sound. Wolff figured out that the volunteers could easily come up with an impression about a person based on how they walked, and the others often agreed. Here are a few statements that participants made about "Subject 45."

- "Dull, somewhat subaltern, insecure."
- "Inwardly insecure try to appear secure to others."
- "Conscious and intentional vanity, eager to be admired."
- "Somebody who wants to gain attention at any price."
- "Pretentious, with no foundation for it."

It's astonishing how they came up with such similar impressions.

But because they had a small sampling, and there was no way to know that they didn't pick up on some other cues, this study has its flaws.

Plus, everybody that participated already knew each other even if they didn't know who they were watching in each video.

Experiments performed now are much more sophisticated. They can now use digital technology to reduce a walk to nothing more than a simple point-light display on a black background using white dots to show the movements of the joints.

This gets rid of any other possible cues.

- Sway or Swing

Using the approach of the black screen and white dots, during the late 80s, US psychologists found there are two types of a walk, which could be described as a youthful or older movement. Youthful movement involves a bouncy movement, the sway of the hips, large arm swings, and frequent stops. Older movements are slower and stiffer with a forward lean.

What's interesting is that their walk didn't always correspond with their age. A person could be young, yet have an older gait and vice versa. Some also assume that people with a younger walk were more powerful and happier. This stayed the same even if their age was apparent by showing their body and face.

This also showed how people made consistent assumptions based on the walking style of people, but they didn't look to see if the assumptions were correct.

To find this out, we need to take a look at a British and Swiss study from a few years back. They had the people rate their own personalities first and compared the assumptions others made based on their walking.

They also came up with two main styles of walking but described them differently. The first walking style is loose and expansive, which was seen as a sign of warmth, trustworthiness, extraversion, and adventurousness. The second was relaxed and slow style, which people saw as emotional stability. But, the judgments based on the walks were wrong. The assumptions didn't match up with what the walker said about their personalities.

- False Assumptions

Our message from this is that we tend to treat a person differently by their walking style just as much as we do based upon their clothing, accent, or looks. This is used as an information source to figure out what kind of person they are. The assumptions made on a person's face tend to be more accurate than the assumption based on their gait.

At least, that is true for the majority of the judgments made based on gait. But we can make a more accurate judgment in a much more sinister way, and it is based upon vulnerability.

In early findings, it was discovered that women and men with a slower walk, smaller arm swing, and shorter stride were seen as vulnerable. In a Japanese study published in 2006, they asked several men how likely it would be that they would inappropriately touch or chat up different females based on their walking styles that were depicted using point-light displays.

The only information they had was their walk, and the men said that they would be more likely to approach a woman who appeared more vulnerable, like coming off as emotionally unstable or introverted. What is worse, prisoners with high psychopathy scores are more accurate at spotting people who have been attacked before simply by watching some video clips of them walking.

There were some prisoners who already knew they had this ability. Those who scored highest in the psychopathy scores stated that they often paid attention to the way that people walked when making a judgment. For example, Ted Bundy is reported having said that he pick out a victim by the way she walked. Now that we know this, let's break down walking styles and what they mean so that you can make accurate judgments.

1. The Multi-tasker

When a person walks, chews gum, and talks at the same time, or other combinations, it shows positive energy. This can also help you when you feel low in energy.

If you start walking around your house while talking and cooking or organizing things, it can give you a boost in creativity. This means if a person often walks like this, then they are highly imaginative.

If you spot a person walking and talking on the phone, and they suddenly stop, the conversation has taken a turn to the serious side. People will most likely stop walking and possibly sit down if the conversation becomes serious.

2. The Stomper

When a person stomps their feet on the ground, it signals their brain about the position of that limb. If a person consistently stomps when they walk, it could mean they have a medical condition. According to Haydn Kelly, a podiatrist, it could be impaired proprioception due to a loss of sensation.

A person who stomps their feet a lot they could have a vitamin B12 deficiency, which can also cause bleeding gums, a sore tongue, and tiredness. This means that a person stomping isn't aggressive if it happens all the time.

3. The Shuffler

A person who constantly shuffles their feet isn't somebody who is lazy but instead is afraid of falling because of changes in the orientation or depth perception. This is common in elderly people but can happen to anybody. Shuffling their feet can end up leading to other medical issues as well.

4. The Arm Swinger

The latissimus dorsi, a muscle, connects our lower back and arms, and because of this muscle, our opposite arm swings when we take a step to help support the low back. The bigger a person's arm swing is, the healthier of a lower back a person has.

If a person has one arm the move more freely than the other, it could indicate that they have a neck or back problem due to inactivity or injury.

5. The Arm Crosser

A person who walks with their arms crossed likely feels vulnerable. If you, yourself, walk this way, you may want to work on correcting this, especially if you are a woman.

Females often cross their arms if they are walking alone at night or in a rough area that they aren't familiar with. Attackers are more likely to prey on people who appear weak, so keeping your arms uncross and standing upright with a quick pace is safer.

6. The Corrector

This person walks light on their toes and keeps their eyes down on the floor. Their pace is cautious and slow as if they are afraid of stepping wrong. They keep their arms close to their side to make sure they don't intrude on other's space. They don't use a phone when they are walking, nor do they interact with friends or others unless they must.

This person is likely polite and introverted. They follow the golden rule of treating others as they want to be treated. Since they are introverted, they don't verbally communicate the things they need or want. They sort of expect people just to know. This can sometimes make then annoyed with other people, and this will make you confused by their irritability. You should expect them to be fairly quiet, and it shouldn't come as a surprise if they act like you are supposed to know exactly what they want.

7. The Supporter

This person's walks with their weight over their legs, not back or forward. They keep a medium-pace, and their movements are very smooth and never choppy. They will engage and gesture to people while they walk, and they like making eye contact instead of shouting or waving. These walkers are often interested in people rather than tasks, and they like enjoying their personal life more than work. They like being a part of a group and do well within a family system or a team. They like to be acknowledged for the things they do, but they won't admit this. They are easily distracted. If you want to impress them, give them a call or send them a card. They have a lot of good qualities, but some people may view them as weak. They have to work hard to stay focused.

8. The Influencer

This person walks with their head held high, shoulders back, and chest out. They also walk quickly with springiness to their step. They like to engage with people they walk past and will often smile, make eye contact, wave, or shout "hello."

Many celebrities and politicians walk this way. These people tend to be socially adept, charismatic, fun, but they do tend to come off as a bit much. They are often over-the-top and hog the spotlight, and they will sometimes take it from others when they shouldn't. They may come off as a bit much, but ultimately, they mean well.

9. The Driver

This person walks with their weight forward and with a quick stride like they are charging forward. These people will sometimes multi-task when they walk, such as talking on the phone. They are great at finding a way around an obstacle. They don't mind bumping into people if they have to.

This person has a lot of positive traits. They are great at getting things done, are productive, logical, and intelligent. They sometimes come off a little cold. They are fiery and competitive, and this can sometimes be their downfall.

This is the most common walk you will see. You may notice a combination of these in some people, but it does give you another way to read what type of person you are dealing with.

Head

The nod of the head means "yes" in almost every place in the world, and shaking the head means "no." A simple nod is most often used a nice greeting, especially if people are far away from one another. It simply lets the person know that "Yes, I see you." The frequency and speed that a person nods with when you are talking with them can share several different messages. A slow nod means that person is listening closely and is interested in what you have to say. A fast nod means they are telling you, "I've heard enough; I want to speak."

You may have even noticed how there are some people who will nod their heads quickly before they interrupt the person who is talking, and then eagerly make a point. If you notice that their head movements contradict their words, then be suspicious. For example, if they say, "That sounds good," but their head is shaking, then they don't actually mean what they say.

When a person's nonverbal signals contradict what they verbally tell you, you should always read what the nonverbal is saying because it tends to be more accurate.

- The Head Tilt

A head tilt suggests that they are interested in the things that you are saying. It's a sign of submission that is often used by women when they are around a person that they like or interested in the conversation.

If you notice a person tilting their head while you are talking, you should know that they either like you, what you are saying or both. To find out which it is, change the topic. If their hand remains tilted, then they are likely interested in more than what you are saying.

The head tilt exposes a very vulnerable part of the body. There are a lot of canines that will lie down and expose their necks when facing a dominant canine to show defeat in order to end the fit without bloodshed or physical aggression.

When a person tilts their head around you, they are telling you, "I trust that you won't harm me." Interestingly, if you make the point of tilting your head as you speak, the listener will trust what you say. This is the reason why many leadership roles and politicians use the support of the head tilt when addressing people.

People will also tilt their head when they look at something that they don't completely understand, like a new gadget or complex painting. When a head tilt happens in this context, they are simply changing the angle of their eyes so that they can get a better view. Make sure you keep the context in mind.

- Chin Positions

The chin in a horizontal position is considered neutral. If the chin is higher than horizontal, they are showing superiority, arrogance, or fearlessness. By raising the chin, the person is trying to appear taller so that they can "look down their nose" at you.

With a raised chin, they are exposing their neck but not in a submissive way. They are, instead, saying, "I dare you to hurt me."

When a person drops their chin below horizontal, it could mean that they are shy, dejected, or sad. They are trying to lower their status and height. This explains the old saying of, "hang your head in shame."

A lowered chin can also mean that they are feeling a deep emotion or engaged in self-talk.

When a person has their chin down and pulled back, they feel judgmental in a negative way or threatened. They make their self look as if they have been hit in the chin by whatever it is that is causing them to feel threatened, so they have it pulled back defensively. This movement also partially hides the vulnerable neck.

This is a very common gesture when a stranger enters a group. The person who starts to feel as if the stranger is going to steal their attention is more likely to do this.

If a person feels disgusted, they will often pull their chin back because they are judging the situation in a negative way.

- The Head Toss

This is another submissive gesture that is often used by women when they are around a person they like. They toss their head back for just a second, flip their hair, and then return their head to a neutral position. Besides showing their neck, this is also used as a way to grab attention by communicating the message of "notice me."

If there is a group of women talking and then an attractive man shows up, you will likely see the women perform the head toss. Women will also do this to get their hair out of their eyes or face while working on something, so make sure you know what the context is before you reach any conclusions.

- Swallowing

When a person hears bad news or is getting ready to something that may not be pleasant, you may notice that the front of their neck moves as if they are swallowing. This swallowing is sometimes accompanied by a short closure of their mouth as if they are really swallowing.

This is really noticeable in men because they usually have a more noticeably Adam's apple. Basically, this type of neck movement signals some type of strong emotion. The majority of the time it signifies fear, something is shows sadness, but there are times when it could be joy or love. When a person is weeping or crying, you will likely see this neck movement often. If there is any situation that makes a person wants to cry, however small, can cause this neck movement.

You will spot this movement right before a doctor tells a family bad news when a person admits that they have made a mistake when a person is afraid that they are going to get caught, and so on. People will make this movement when they have tears of joy as well or when they tell somebody they love them.

- Shaking and Nodding

Nodding movements are a sign of agreement in most cultures and are likely accompanied by smiling and other approval signs. A vigorous nod typically shows strong agreement. A slow nod could mean a conditional agreement.

When a person shakes their head, it typically means that they don't agree or they disapprove in some way. The speed of this shake indicates how strong their feeling is. When a person tilts their head down while they shake, it could mean a certain type of disapproval.

When somebody tilts their head from side to side often means "I'm not sure." In Southern India, this movement means yes.

A person that nods their head while you talk shows encouragement and that they want you to continue talking. If they shake their head while you talk shows disagreement and they may end up stopping you.

A person can use a nod to emphasize their point. This can be a subtle nod or an aggressive and rapid tilt. A quick sharp nod can show a head-butt, meaning that they would like to strike the other person.

Arms

Whether you cross your arms to protect yourself or open them to welcome a person, the way your arms are positioned shares a lot of information with a watchful observer.

There are certain arm positions that create certain moods. Crossed arms keep your feelings held in and other's out. They show that a person has created roadblocks that another person can't travel past. If you hold a position for too long, you are going to start feeling negative and shut off. Unless, a person is cold, in which case keeping your arms crossed is just helping to keep your warm and is perfectly normal.

As far as contact goes, touching can help be restorative as long as you considered how, where, when, and who to do it too. If touching is done correctly, it helps to connect and engage with a person. If it is done wrong, things can turn ugly. Let's go through a few different signals to watch out for when you meet somebody.

- Barrier Signals

Trying to find a barrier to hide behind is normal, and we learn this skill at a very young age in order to protect yourself. Children often hide behind anything that appears to be solid, such as a parent, couches, or table legs if they start to feel threatened in some way. As we get older, this turns into more sophisticated actions because it becomes unacceptable to hide behind solid objects. This is why we begin to cross our arms if we start to feel threatened.

This continues to develop throughout our adulthood to the point that others don't even notice it. By crossing one or both arms over our chest, we are creating an unconscious barrier to try and block other things that we don't like or view as threatening. The reason we fold our arms like this is that it protects the lungs and heart; we want to protect these vital organs from attack.

Chimps and monkeys also cross their arms to help protect against a frontal attack. This means that if a person walks up to you with their arms crossed, you can about guarantee that they have a defensive, negative, or nervous attitude.

- Problems with Crossed Arms

There has research performed into the gesture of arms crossed, and it has found some interesting results. In one study, a group of students was asked to go to a lecture series where they had to sit with their arms and legs uncrossed through the whole thing. Afterward, they were tested to see how much they ended up learning and the views that they had created towards the speaker. They asked another group of students to go to the same lecture, but they were told to have their arms crossed.

They ended up discovering that the ones they had to keep their arms crossed learned 40% less than the one that kept their arms uncrossed. The second group had created more critical opinions of the lecturer and lectures and found the lecturer to be less credible.

Years ago, another study was performed in a similar manner with 1500 lecture attendees, and they had almost identical results. They discovered that those who sat with their arms fold created negative impressions about the speaker, and they didn't pay attention to what was being said.

This is why many training centers have chosen to use chairs with armrests so that the attendees can be comfortable with their arms uncrossed.

- It's Comfortable

You can ask people about why they have their arms crossed, and many will say it comfortable. The truth is, any gesture will feel comfortable only if you have the right attitude.

This means that if you are feeling nervous, defensive, or negative, having folded arms are going to feel comfortable. If you are out with your friends having, then folded arms aren't going to feel right.

With any body language, the message it sends depends on the sender and receiver. You might feel "comfortable" if you have your arms crossed with your neck and back stiff, but studies have found that other people react to these gestures in a negative way.

So, this means that not only does another person having crossed arms mean that they are already in a negative headspace, you should also try to avoid crossing your arms if you want to show others that you agree.

- Differences by Gender

The rotation of our arms depends on our gender. Men's arms will rotate slightly inward, but a woman will rotate slightly outwards.

This slight bodily difference is the reason mean can throw more accurately, and women have a more stable elbow to hold a baby. Something that is interesting is that women tend to have their arms open when a person is around them that they view as attractive, and they cross their arms if they don't think a person is attractive.

- Crossed over The Chest

Both arms crossed over the chest is a barrier to block a person they don't like. There are actually many different arms-folded positions that people can take that mean slightly different things. This gesture, with the arms over the chest, is universal and should be read with the same negative or defensive meaning in nearly every country. Strangers in a public meeting use this; people in queue lines will do this as well. Basically, any place where a person feels insecure or uncertain.

A lot of people will make this gesture when they disagree with what a person is saying. Speakers that haven't picked up on this position in their listeners won't be able to communicate their message. The experienced speaker knows that they need to use an ice breaker to get their audience into a receptive position so that their attitude moves from negative to positive.

When a person takes this position, it may be safe to assume that you have said something that they don't agree with. It could be pointless to continue on with your argument even if they verbally agree with you. Body language can be trusted more than words.

You need to work towards figuring out the reason for the crossed arms and try to get them into an open position. Their attitude creates this gesture, and then keeping the gesture keeps the attitude around.

A good way to try and get a person to release this arms-folded position is to ask them to hold something or give them a task to perform.

If you provide them with a refreshment, brochure, or pen, it makes them have to uncross their arms and lean towards you. This places them in a more receptive position.

Asking them to lean forward so that they can look at a presentation can be an effective way of opening them up. Alternatively, you can also lean forwards keeping your palms face up, and then say, "I noticed that you might have a question. What do you want to know?" Then sit back so that they can clearly see that you want them to talk. When you have your palms face up, you are showing them that you would like them to be honest with you.

Negotiators and salespeople are taught that they shouldn't continue with a presentation until the person has unfolded their arms. Buyers often already have created some sort of object that a salesperson probably won't discover because they didn't notice their arms.

A person who has their fists clenched and their arms crossed over their chest shows hostility and defensiveness. If this is coupled with clenched teeth or a tight-lipped smile and a red face, or they verbally say something aggressive, a physical attack could be imminent.

- Gripped Arms

This gesture is where a person tightly grips their upper arms with their hands. This is to reinforce their self and avoid exposing the front of their body.

Some will grip their arms so tight that their knuckles turn white. This is a form of a self-comforting hug. This is often seen in people in a waiting room or for people who are traveling by plane for the first time. It shows that they have a restrained, negative attitude.

- Subordinates and Managers

Status often influences crossed arms. A person who is higher in their social class can make their preeminence known by keeping their arms unfolded. This basically tells people, "I'm the one in control."

Let's say that you are at a company function and your manager is introducing new employees. He shakes their hand and then steps back to a normal spacing after introductions have been made. His hands will then go down by his sides, in his pockets, or behind him. Rarely does he ever fold his arms over his chest so that he never shows nervousness?

But, once the new employees shake his hand, they may fully or partially cross their arms because of the apprehension of being in the presence of a manager. Both the new employees and the manager feel completely comfortable with the gestures they have chosen as the signal of their status.

How do you think things would play out if a manager comes up to a new, confident employee who thinks that he is just as important as the manager?

There's a good chance that after greeting with a strong handshake, he steps back and crosses arms and keeps his thumbs up.

The thumbs pointed up gestures shows that the person feels as if they are in control of their situations. Whenever they talk, they likely gesture with their thumbs to emphasize a point they are making.

By having their arms crossed, they are creating some protection, but their thumbs up is also showing that they are very confident.

A person who feels submissive to who they are talking with, or defensive, will sit symmetrically. This means that both sides of their body will mirror each other.

They will appear tenser and will often look as if they are expecting to be attacked. If a person feels defensive and dominant, they will be asymmetrically posed, meaning both sides of their body are positioned differently.

- Thumbs-Up

If you are telling somebody something and they cross their arms with their thumbs up once you finished, and they are also showing other positive cues, it would be safe to ask them for some type of commitment or agreement. But, if instead they cross their arms and clench their fists, you might not want to try to get them to agree to something or to say yes. It would be better if you start asking them questions in order to uncover their objections. Once a person has said no, it tends to be hard to change their mind without coming off as aggressive. Being able to read their body language gives you a chance to spot their negativity before having them verbalize it, and then you take a different course of action.

Historically, people who were wearing armor or carrying weapons didn't use these types of gestures because they had armor or a weapon to protect them.

- Half Hugs

As a child, you likely received hugs from your parents or caregiver whenever you faced a tense or distressing circumstance.

As an adult, you likely try to recreate this comfort when in a stressful situation. Instead of completely crossing your arms, which suggests fearfulness or anxiety, women will often use an understated half-hug where only one arm is crossed over their body in order to touch or hold the other arm.

These single-arm barriers are seen in situations where a person views their self as a newcomer to a group or doesn't have much self-confidence.

- The Fig Leaf

This gesture is where they clasp both hands over the lower stomach.

If a person is placed into a vulnerable positive, but they know they need to come off as confident and respectful, they will likely stand with their hands clasped over their crotch or lower stomach.

You can see this gesture used by politicians and any other types of leaders or people who are subjected to the public eye. This might be seen during social meetings that are presided over by an authority figure, like a priest giving a sermon.

Men will hold this position to feel secure by covering their genitals. They are subconsciously protecting their self from an attack. Don't allow yourself to be fooled into believing that this is a natural, confident position.

This position feels comfortable because it creates a shield. This is often a position that people take when they are in line for food at a homeless shelter or receiving unemployment because they feel vulnerable. Adolf Hitler stood like this a lot in public to mask his sexual inadequacy.

- How Important People Show Insecurities

People who are constantly in the public eye, like actors, politicians, and royalty, typically don't want others to notice that they are unsure or nervous.

They want to come off as controlled, calm, and cool when out in public, but they still leak out their apprehension or anxiety in some disguised arm-crossing.

This works like any other arms-crossed gesture, one arm crosses over in front of the body to the other arm, but they don't fully cross their arms. Instead, they grab hold of a cuff, bracelet, watch, purse, or anything else that is close to their other arm. They are still forming a barrier in order to feel secure.

Men with cufflinks will often be seen adjusting the cufflinks as they walk across a room where they are on full display of the other guests.

You can spot a self-conscious or anxious man by seeing if he messes with a button, adjusts his watch, checks his wallet, rubs his hands together, or anything else that gives him the ability to reach an arm in front of his body.

Business people often go into meetings holding a laptop or briefcase in front of their body. To a person who knows what to look for, this is a signal of nervousness because this position doesn't do or show anything else.

You can easily spot these types of things in areas where people have to walk past others that are watching them. You can't spot a woman's disguised arm barriers as easily as a man's because they often carry a purse that can be grasped to hide their self-consciousness, but it appears as if they are simply holding their purse.

- Objects as Barriers

If a person places a laptop, a cup, or any other object between them and you, they are trying to create a protective barrier.

These are subconscious efforts of trying to conceal their insecurity or nervousness, whether they are aware of it or not.

If you are somewhere where they are serving drinks, people will hold their cup in front of them in both hands to create a barrier that they can hide behind.

- Amiability

When arms are open, it means that a person is honest, friendly, and receptive. This shows that they aren't hiding anything and that you can easily approach them. This makes others feel comfortable and ease and will draw people in.

When people make sure that their body is exposed, it let's other people know that they are open and receptive to whatever has to be said.

Open arms let people know that they are constructive and confident and makes the environment more positive.

This person is trustworthy, direct, and sincere, as long as their other gestures remain equally forthright and open.

- Embracing

When you are at the airport, watch how family and friends hug when people arrive or depart. When a person hugs on arrival, the embrace is longer than it is when they are leaving. When they first see each other, the hugs are very intense and have a strong embrace.

They are bringing each other into their personal space. A departure hug is less passionate and short. It's as if that since they are saying goodbye, they have to release each other.

If a person pats your back when hugging, they are letting you the hug has gone on long enough.

Legs

When a body part is far away from our head, we are less aware of what it does. This means that we have more control over our facial expressions. Most people can give you a fake frown or smile. The one area of our body that we are the least aware of is our feet and legs.

This means that this area is where we can get the most information about a person because they are less aware of what those body parts are doing. While their face may appear composed, a restless foot lets you know otherwise.

There are four main standing positions that a person takes:

1. Parallel

This stance is a subordinate stance where the feet are close together, and the legs are straight. This is a neutral and formal standing attitude. In a school setting, children will often stand in this manner when they speak with their teacher. People who are facing a judge will often stand like this, or if they have to meet with their commanding officer.

When feet are close together, it reduces the foundation and makes the stance precarious. A person can be easily pushed over when they are in this position if caught off guard. People who are unsure will often take this stance. With their legs close, they are showing that they feel hesitant.

2. Legs Apart

This is mainly a male gesture and is a stable posture. It shows you that the person is standing their ground. They are showing their dominance.

This is where they keep their legs straight and have the feet positions hip-width apart so that the weight is equally distributed between both legs.

Since men have a higher center of gravity, they will adopt this stance more often than women. Besides their height, men take this position more often around other people when they are using their posture to communicate.

It signals dominance by men because it highlights their genitals, which makes them look virile. In sporting events, you will often see men standing in this position.

3. Foot Forward Pose

Between the Middle Ages and the 19th century, the high society men used a stance that would show off their inner leg, which they viewed as an erotic part of the body.

They stood where their weight was supported by the back leg, and they had their other leg kicked out in front of them to show off their inner thigh. The fashion during those times made it more possible to show off their masculinity and legs. You will see celebrities on the red carpet do this.

This is a good indication to what a person's intentions are because we all point our lead foot towards what is on our mind, and this stance also gives the impression that a person is getting ready to walk.

When in a group, a person's lead foot points at the most attractive or interesting person, but when they want to leave, they will point that foot to the closest exit.

4. Cross-Legged

This is a standing cross-legged position. The next time you are at a meeting where there are men and women, you will likely see some people standing with the legs and arms crossed.

If you look a bit more closely, you are going to notice that they are standing further apart from each than is customary.

This is how a lot of people will stand when they are around people who they don't know all that well. If you took a moment to ask them a few questions, you would probably find out that most of them were strangers until that moment.

When legs are open, it means dominance and openness, but when legs are crossed, it shows a closed attitude or defensiveness because it symbolically denies the other person access to the genitals.

- The Leg Cross

We're moving on from standing to stead positions. 70% of people who sit with their legs crossed will place the left over their right. This is a normal position used by the majority of Asians and Europeans. If a person has their limbs crossed, they are pulling themselves out of the conversation, and it is likely going to be a waste of your time to convince them of something that they have pushed out of their mind.

- Figure Four

If you look down at this seated cross-legged position, it will look like the number. Instead of completely crossing the leg over, they prop it on top of the other leg. This is commonly using among American men. This likely shows a person who feels competitive or argumentative.

While this is less common in Europe, there are more cultures adopting it around the world. It is common for men to sit like this in order to appear youthful and relaxed. In places like the Middle East and parts of Asia, this seated position is seen as an insult because it exposes the bottom of the shoes, which they see as filthy.

Women in pants will often sit like this, but they typically only do it around other women. They don't want to chance coming off as too masculine by doing this around men.

- Leg Clamp

This is a figure four with the hands clasped on the top leg. This shows that they are competitive, and it also lets you know that they are stubborn and will likely reject anything that you try to tell them that goes against what they already believe.

- Locked Ankles

In many body language studies performed by Henry Calero and Gerard Nierenberg, a person sitting with their ankles locked tend to be hiding information.

Airline personnel are trained to look for this because this shows a person who needs something but is too shy to ask. Apprehensive travelers sit like this, especially at take-off.

In other studies, they looked at patients in a dental office. Of 150 men, 128 of them immediately crossed the ankles when they sat down in the dentist's chair. They would also either grip the armrests or clasp their hands over their groin. They also studied 150 women. Of those, 90 would sit with the ankles crossed and place their hands over the midsection.

- Seated Parallel Legs

The bone structure of women's hips and legs gives them the ability to sit like this in order to project strong feminine signals.

A man can't comfortably replicate this position. When surveyed, men say this is their favorite seated position for women.

- Fidgeting Feet

When a person's feet fidget, they are likely reaching their impatience threshold. Their feet are telling you that they want to get away and so they have to fidget until they get the chance to. When standing, repeatedly tapping their foot shows impatience. If seated with their legs crossed, twitching the foot up and down shows impatience.

Chapter 3:
Non-Verbal Language How the Brain Controls Body Language

The reason nonverbal language never lies is that it happens unconsciously. We have the ability to consciously control the things we say in order to lie or share half-truths, but the body will still show the truth, why does this happen?

Humans have evolved to communicate in a nonverbal manner. There is an ancient system that lives inside our brain that understands and conveys intentions or emotions through physical movements.

This part of the brain is what is called the limbic system. It works in a precise manner. The amygdala is the key player in the limbic system and is located in the medial temporal lobe. It works by helping us to process emotions.

There is an interesting evolutionary story that explains how the limbic system cam to be. It takes us through how water-dwelling creatures became land roaming and continues to turn into walking, talking, and hunting humans.

Something that is hard to believe for most is that creatures have evolved from common ancestors. These ancestors lived in the water 360 million years ago. The struggle to survive and climatic changes forced them to move to the land. Their fins turned into limbs in order to walk, and their skin became tougher in order to handle the harsh climate.

About 320 to 310 million years ago, the reptile evolved. This was when the limbic system began to develop. The reflexive system of the breed, feed, flight, and the fight began. The part of the brain this created consisted of the cerebellum and brain stem. The behavior of the reptile is predictable, but it is what helped them to survive. Emotions didn't exist until mammals evolved.

When mammals emerged, they had a deliberate social behavior, unlike their reptile ancestors. The reason for this could be connected to their habitation, bonding, nurturing, reproduction, and changed metabolism. A mammal's offspring grows inside of them until they reach a certain stage. They are feed by secretions from the mammary glands, and they control their temperature in order to adjust to different climates. The new brain structure, called the cortex, for mammals was built upon the reptilian complex. This new brain section consisted of the insula, orbital frontal cortex, cingulate gyrus, hippocampus, and amygdala. Even though mammals were superior in their survival, they naturally used the fight or flight approach, which is a reptilian act. They created other ways to work around this fight or flight approach through planned movements, expressions, and behavior. Emotions were a great gift as well as being able to smell different things and being able to remember them. This helped mammals to endure different circumstances. This caused them to spread across the planet.

Finally, the common ancestors of apes and humans appeared the primate. It is possible that they evolved from mammals that were more skilled at climbing trees for shelter and food. The primate's brain developed more complex parts to help them adapt to new environments and social challenges. They have better systems to coordinate movements on the ground and in trees. They had the ability to plan and think. Their vision also improved, and they could recall scenes.

As the climate changed, parts of these primates remained in wooded areas, leaving in the trees. Others were forced to start roaming the ground when their trees were replaced by brush. These primates start to walk on two legs with the hands-free to farm, fish, hunt, make tools and gather food. They start to build and live in fixed shelters.

This ability to walk on two feet changed their movement and behavior patterns and how they communicated. Making different sounds, gestures, and facial expressions became helpful in express their feelings to the other people in their group. Through various civilizations, this continues to be a diverse part of their lifestyle and communication. This created their cultural and social norms and ethics.

For us, modern humans, the neocortex is the most advanced part of the brain. This rests above all of the old brain sections. This section of the brain is the reason why we can solve problems, figure out math, navigate our way around, perform introspection, learn other languages, use our imagination, and reason things. This is also the area that helps us to regulate our emotions, harbor feelings, and control a few of the impulses of our limbic system. The limbic brain is what controls all of our nonverbal communication, and we can't completely control it with our neocortex.

Emotional and visual memory has the ability to cause us to act in ways that our ancestors would. We feel comfortable in favorable situations and uncomfortable when in danger or distress. When we are placed in a threatening situation, we are still going to act like other mammals or reptiles.

Chapter 4
Non Verbal Signals

Being able to communicate well is a very important part of succeeding in the professional and personal world, but it's not the words you say that scream.

Rather, it is your body language. Your eye contact, tone of voice, posture, gestures, and facial expressions are your best communication tools.

They have the ability to undermine, confuse, offend, draw others in, build trust, or put people at ease.

There are a lot of times where what a person says and what their body language says is completely different. Nonverbal communication can do five things:

- Accent – It can underline or accent your verbal message.

- Complement – It can complement or add to what you are verbally saying.

- Substitute – It can be used in place of a verbal message.

- Contradict – It can go against what you are verbally trying to say making your listener think you are lying.

- Repeat – It can strengthen and repeat your verbal message.

There are several different forms of nonverbal communication that we will look at in this chapter. We will cover:

- Facial expressions – As you will learn, the face is expressive and is able to express several emotions without saying one word. Unlike the things we say and other forms of body language, facial expressions are often very universal.

- Posture and body movement – Take a moment to think about how you view people based on how they hold their head , walk around, stand, and sit. The way a person carries their self provides a lot of information.

- Gestures – These are woven into our life. You speak animatedly; argue with your hands, beckon, point, and wave. However, gestures vary across cultures.

- Eye contact – Since sight tends to be the strongest sense for most people, it is an important part of nonverbal communication. The way a person looks at, you can tell you whether they are attracted to you, hostile, affectionate, or interested. It also helps conversations to flow.

Nonverbal communication can wrong in many different ways. It is quite easy to confuse different signals, but the rest of this chapter will ensure that this won't happen.

The Lower Body

The arms can share a lot of information. The hands can share more, but the legs provide us with the exclamation point and tell users exactly what a person is thinking. The legs can tell you if a person is comfortable and open. They can also show dominance or show where they actually want to go.

- Feet Pointing

Watch the direction of a person's feet to find out where their attention is. The feet will always point towards what is on a person's mind or what they are focusing on. Everybody has a lead foot, depending on the dominant hand. When a person that we are interested in is talking, the lead food will point toward them. However, if a person would like to leave a situation they are in, you will see their foot pointing towards an exit or how they would like to go. If a person is seated during a conversation, look at where their feet are pointed to see what they are actually interested.

- Shy Tangle

This tends to be something that women do more often than men, but anybody who starts to feel timid or shy will something entangle their legs crossing them under and over to try and block out bad emotions and make themselves look small. There is another shy leg twirl that people can do while standing. The actual act of this movement is crossing one leg over the other and hooking that foot behind the knee as if they are trying to scratch an itch.

- Smarty Pants

This is a very apparent position where a person tries to make their self-look bigger. They are typically seated with the legs splayed open and leaned back. They may even spread their arms out and lock them behind their head. This is often used by those who are feeling confident, superior, or dominant.

- Touching

A person, when standing, can only touch their thighs or bottom. They can do this in a seductive manner, or they can slap their legs as if saying, "Let's go." It can also indicate irritation. This is where paying attention to the context of the conversation is important.

The Upper Body

The upper body language will often show signs of defensive signs because the arms can easily be used as a shield, as discussed above. But upper body language also involves the chest. Let's go through some language of the upper body.

- The Superman

This is a common move by models, bodybuilders, and was made popular by Superman. This can have many different meanings depending on how a person uses it. In the animal world, animals try to make their self-look bigger when they feel threatened.

If you watch a house cat, when they get spooked, they stretch their legs, and their fur stands on end. Humans also have this, even though it isn't as noticeable. This is why we get goosebumps.

Since we can't make our self-look bigger anymore, we have come up with arm gestures like placing our hands on our waist. This shows us that a person is getting ready to act assertively.

This is common in athletes before a game, or a wife nagging at her spouse. A guy who is flirting with a girl will sue this to appear assertive. This is what is referred to as a readiness gesture.

- Chest Thrust Outward

If a person pushes their chest out, they are trying to draw attention to that part of them, and it can also be used a type of romantic display.

Women understand that men are programmed to become aroused by breasts. When you notice a woman pushing her chest out, she may be inviting intimate relations.

Men thrust their chest out to show off their chest and possibly to hide their gut. The difference is men do this to women and other men.

- Profiled Chest

If a person is standing sideways or angled at 45 degrees, they are trying to accentuate the thrust-out chest. Women may do this to show off the curve of their breasts, and men do this to show off their profile.

- Leaning

If a person leans forward, it moves them closer to the other person. There are two meanings to this. First, it tells you that they are interested in something, which could just be what you are saying. Bu, this movement can also show romantic interest.

Second, a lean forward can invade personal space, hence showing themselves as a threat. This is often an aggressive display. This is an unconscious thing that powerful people will do.

The Hands

The human hands have 27 bones, and they are an expressive part of our bodies. This gives us a lot of capability to handle our environment.

Reading palms isn't about looking at the lines on the hands. After a person's face, the hands are the best source for body language.

Gestures of the hands vary greatly across cultures, and one hand gesture might be innocent in one country but offensive in another.

Hand signals might be small, but the show what our subconscious is thinking. A gesture might be exaggerated and done using both hands to show a point.

- Shaping

The hands have the ability to cut our words into the air to emphasize the things that we are saying and our meaning. They are trying to create a visualization out of nothing.

If a man is trying to describe a fish he caught on his fishing trip; he might try to show the shape by indicating with his hands. He could also carve out a specific shape that he would like his ideal mate to be. Other gestures might be cruder when they hold certain body parts and move sexually.

- Holding

A person with cupped hands is indicating they can gently hold onto something. They show delicacy or holding onto something fragile. Hands that are gripping show desire, ownership, or possessiveness. The tighter their fist is, the stronger they are feeling an emotion.

If a person is holding their own hands, they are trying to comfort themselves. They could also be trying to restrain themselves, so they allow someone else to talk. It might be used if they are angry, and it is keeping them from attacking. If they are wringing their hands, they are feeling very nervous.

Holding their hands behind their back shows they are confident by opening up their front. They might conceal their hands to hide their tension. If one hand is holding onto the other arm, the tighter and higher the grip, the more they are tense. Two hands could show different desires. If one is forming a fist with the other one holding it back, it might be showing that they want to punch someone.

A person who is lying tries to control their hands. If they hold them still, you might want to get suspicious. Remember that these are only indicators, and you need to look for other signals.

If a person looks like they are holding an object like a cup or pen, this shows they are trying to comfort themselves. If a person is holding a cup, but they are holding it close where it looks like they are "hugging" the cup, they are hugging themselves. Holding onto an item using both hands makes a closed position.

Items could be used as a distraction to release nervous energy like holding a pen but doodling, clicking it off and on or fiddling with it.

If their hands are clenched together in front of them but relaxed, with their thumbs resting on to could show pleasure.

- Greeting

Our hands are used to greet others. The most common is the handshake. Opening of the palm shows they don't have any concealed weapons. This is used when waving, salutes, and greetings.

This is a time when we get to touch another person, and it could send many different signals.

Dominance is indicated by shaking hands and placing another one on top. How strong and how long they shake your hands tells you that they are deciding on when to stop the handshake.

Affection can be shown with the duration and speed of the handshake, smiles, and touching with the other hand. The similarity between this one and dominant can lead to situations when a dominant person tries to pretend they are friendly.

Submission is shown by a palm up, a floppy handshake that is sometimes clammy and comes with fast withdrawal.

Many handshakes will use vertical palms that show equality. They will be firm but not crushing and for an exact amount of time, so both parties know when they need to let go.

Waving is an easy way to greet somebody and can easily be performed from far away.

Salutes are usually only done by the military, where the style is prescribed.

- Control

If they are holding their hands with the palms facing downward might be figuratively restraining or holding onto someone else. This might be an authoritative action telling you to stop now or it might be a request asking you to calm down. This will appear with the dominant hand placed on a top handshake. If they are leaning on their desk with their palms down, it usually shows dominance. If their palms are facing outward toward another person might be them trying to push them away or trying to fend them off. They could be saying, "stop, don't come closer."

If they are pointing their finger or whole hand, they might be telling a person to leave now.

The Face

A person's facial expressions can help us figure out if we believe or trust what they are saying. The most trustworthy expression will have a slight smile and a raised eyebrow. This expression shows confidence and friendliness.

We often make judgments about how intelligent someone is by their facial expressions. People who have a narrow face and a prominent nose were thought to be very intelligent. People who smile and have joyous expressions can be judged as being intelligent rather than a person who looks angry.

- Eyes

Many people refer to the eyes as being the "window to the soul" because they can reveal a lot about what we are thinking and feeling. While you talk with someone, take note of their eye movements. Some things you might notice is whether they are making eye contact, looking down, how quickly they are blinking or if they have dilated pupils

1. Size of Pupils

This can be a very subtle signal. The light level within the environment can change the pupil dilation, but emotions could cause changes in the pupil size. You might have heard the expression "bedroom eyes." If a person's eyes are very dilated, they could be aroused or very interested.

2. Blinking

This is a natural bodily function, but you need to pay attention to whether or not a person blinks too little or too much. People that blink rapidly might indicate they are feeling uncomfortable or distressed. When a person doesn't blink enough, they may be trying to control how their eyes move. Someone playing poker might blink less because they are trying to look unexcited about the hand they were dealt with.

3. Eye Gaze

When a person looks at you as you two are talking, they are paying attention and showing interest. Prolonged eye contact might feel threatening. If you break eye contact and look away quickly could indicate that they are trying to hide their real feelings, uncomfortable, or distracted

- Mouth

Mouth movements and expressions are needed when trying to read body language. Chewing on the lower lip might indicate a person is feeling insecure, fear, or worry.

If they cover their mouth, it might indicate they are trying to be polite if they are coughing or yawning. It could be an attempt to cover up disapproval. Smiling is the best body signal, but smiles could be interpreted in several ways. Smiles can be genuine, or they might be used to show cynicism, sarcasm or false happiness.

Look out for the following:

1. Mouth Turned Down or Up

Changes in the mouth that are subtle could be an indicator of how a person might be feeling. If their mouth is turned up slightly, they might be feeling optimistic or happy. If their mouth is turned down, they might be feeling disapproval, sadness or grimacing.

2. Covering Their Mouth

If a person wants to hide a reaction, they might cover their mouth trying to hide a smirk or smile.

3. Biting Their Lip

People might bite their lip when they are feeling stressed, anxious, or worried.

4. Their Lips are Pursed

If a person tightens their lips, it might be showing distrust, disapproval, or distaste.

Signs of Negative Emotions

The silent signals you show might harm your business without you realizing it. We have over 250,000 facial signals and

700,000 body signals. Having poor body language could damage your relationships by sending other people to signal that you can't be trusted. They could alienate, turn off, or offend others. You need to keep your body language in check, and this takes a lot of effort. Most of the tie, you might not know you are doing it and you could be hurting yourself and your business. In order to help you manage your signals, there are several body languages and speech mistakes that you can learn to prevent. Here are 14 mistakes you need to try to avoid:

1. Too Strong or Weak Handshake

Handshakes are usually the first impression that somebody gets from you. If your handshake is too weak, it shows you aren't professional and might be new. If your handshake is too strong, it might warn them that you are too aggressive. Try to seek out a happy medium so that you can make a good impression.

2. Looking Around

Everyone has encountered somebody who constantly looked around the room while talking with you. It probably made you think they were trying to find another person to talk to. Don't be this type of person. Everybody you talk to need to be treated with respect.

3. Not Smiling

Do you realize that smiling can actually make you feel happy? People like to believe the opposite. If you can keep a nice smile plastered on your face, you will feel confident and people will be glad to work with you. If you catch yourself wanting to make a face, turn that into a smile.

4. No Eye Contact

I used to work with a person who would immediately stare into space anytime somebody talked to them. They said it was easier for them to focus on what others were saying if they didn't look at the talker. People use many diverse communication types but always try to smile and make eye contact.

Even keeping moderate eye contact communicates interest, confidence, and will put everyone at ease.

5. Scrunched-Up Face

You might not know that having a scrunched-up face and furrowed brow might make others think you are hostile or intimidating.

This can discourage a person from being open, or it can cause them to become defensive. You can verbally assure them that you support and understand what they are saying.

6. Looking at Your Phone

If you are at a public gathering, put your phone away. Everyone is addicted to their phones now, but it is very rude. Try to engage with others and stop checking your phone every five minutes. If you have an emergency, that is fine. It is a lot easier to make a connection if something isn't distracting you.

7. Slumping

A person that slumps in their seat shows that they lack in confidence or energy. It is important to show some passion and allow others to know that you believe in yourself.

If you are slumping or hunched over, it is sending the wrong message. If you have a strong posture, you will feel energetic and it will be a win for everyone involved.

8. Not Listening

It doesn't matter what line of work you are in. You are going to have to talk with people some time or other. The main thing that will break or make a relationship is not listening.

Listening can impact your relationship with suppliers, employee performance, and sales better than other forms of communications.

9. Speaking too Fast

Blinking quickly or speaking too fast shows distrust and nervousness. Try to pause between each sentence and allow others to finish their sentences before interrupting. Eye contact is extremely important. If you have a hard time looking people in the eye, look at the middle of their forehead. It resembles eye contact without the uncomfortable feelings.

10. Getting in Their Personal Space

Invading another person's personal space has detrimental effects. A good example is men seem always to invade a woman's personal space whether they know it or not. This can cause harassment lawsuits. The best space to keep between you and another person is about half a foot. Don't treat another person's space as your own.

11. Using "But"

Repeatedly using the word "but" while talking can cause problems. Most of the time, this is going to make it seem like you are trying to make up excuses or like you don't care about what another person is saying. You might say: "I am sorry that your product didn't get to you one time, but you know how the weather is." This statement doesn't show you are truly sorry. You are putting the blame on the weather rather than addressing the person's problem.

12. Not Enough Response

If you are talking with a person, be sure to listen. This means you need to smile, nod, and make eye contact.

Even when two people don't agree with each other is saying, you should still let the other person know that you heard what they said.

This is simply showing them respect. If you don't do this, you are leaving a bad impression. By observing others carefully, you can detect emotions from non-verbal signals.

These indicators are in no way a guarantee. Contextual clues might be used, in addition to what the person is saying and what is happening around you.

Here are some emotions and how to recognize them:

- Embarrassment

False smiles

Grimacing

Changing the topic or trying to cover up their embarrassment

Face or neck is flushed or red

Looking away or down

Not making eye contact

- Anger

Using power body language

Face or neck is flushed or red

Use of aggressive body language

Snarling or baring their teeth

Leaning forward

Invading body space

Fists are clenched

- Sadness

Tears

Body drooping

The flat tone of voice

Lips trembling

- Nervousness, anxiety, and fear

Fear can happen when our basic needs get threatened. There are several levels of fear. It might be mild anxiety or all the way to blind terror. The various bodily changes that are created by fear make this one easy to see.

Any symptoms of stress

Breaking out in a cold sweat

Fight or flight body language

Face is pale

Body language is defensive

Dry mouth indicated by rubbing their throat, drinking water, or licking their lips

Fidgeting

Not looking at others

Gasping or holding their breath

Eyes are damp

Muscle tension such as legs wrapped around something, jerky movements, elbows are drawn in, clenched arms or hands

Lips trembling

Sweating

Vocal tone variations

Pulse rate very high

Errors in speech

Voice trembling

Signs of Positive Emotions

Positive body language means you are approachable, interested, and open.

This doesn't mean that people should use this type of body language at all times or that it is even the best group of signs that show a person is friendly, it is just a good starting point for reading positivity in yourself and others.

- Becoming too Positive

Just because you have positive body language does not mean it is good or the best way to communicate. Because we are social animals, we have many attitudes and emotions.

If you try just to use one at a time, you will seem one dimensional or fake. Expressing attentive and positive attitudes at all times could hurt your status and reputation.

People will often start to take this for granted and will dismiss this. You should give attention and care to others but just to the people who deserve it.

This holds true for anyone who wants to be extra nice to the person they are dating. How can others take care of you, if you only try to help others and dismiss yourself, you will appear shallow and boring. There won't be any excitement or tension.

- Leaning Forward

When a person likes somebody, they want to get close to them. You will seem more interesting if you get closer to them. When a person leans, and especially if they are smiling and nodding, it shows that they are interested in the things that you are saying and would like you to continue. Does this mean you always need to nod and lean forward?

No, overdoing this might cause two problems:

1. If you lean too far, you could invade their personal space and cause them to feel uncomfortable. This is another reason we lean forward when we want to intimidate an opponent. This type of lean will be more aggressive and tenser.

2. If you constantly lean and smile with everyone, you will appear like you are very eager to please. You will lower your status with others.

Compare leaning to driving. When you press on the gas pedal, the more eager and engaged, you are. If you don't press on the pedal, you will appear more distant and relaxed. Don't go toward the extreme because you will need to change your speed for each situation.

Much like with driving, the direction in which a person leans has a big impact. We will gesture and lean toward things or places we want.

- Nothing to Hide

Think about a time when you were away from your friends or family for an extended period of time. How did they greet you when they saw you again? Did they spread the arms and expose their palms like they were hugging you from a distance?

This positive and open gesture can warm your heart. Even though you can't use it daily with everybody, your boss may think your mind has left you, or you have won the lottery.

You can use gestures that are similar to show positive, honest, and open body language.

When the palms are faced outward, this shows a sign of honesty and willingness and is not threatening in any way. You are letting the other person know that you aren't hiding anything and that they can trust you.

Here are some other signals that might help show cooperation and sincerity:

1. Smile

2. Keep your body straight to show energy and confidence

3. Keep your clothes and body open. Don't hold anything in front of you.

4. Have good eye contact. This shows you aren't afraid but are being attentive.

5. Put your hands in a position that is neutral. Never look down on them or bow to their wishes.

- Stay Away from Barriers

In order to gain a person's trust, you have to make sure that you don't come off as a threat and that you don't see them as a threat.

Having defensive body language can affect your attitude. If you are defensive, it is going to make it hard for other people to accept and approach you.

For this main reason, you have to keep open body language and stay away from barriers. Your goal needs to be getting rid of your defenses and to make a confident, warm, and welcoming atmosphere.

Show others that you aren't scared of them and they don't need to be afraid of you either.

This is a process, and total strangers aren't going to be your biggest fan. If you understand what steps to take, you can know their attitude toward you and speed things up.

The steps are as follows:

1. Total strangers will probably have their legs or arms crossed or possibly both. They will stay away from you. They might also hold something in front of them or button their coat.

2. As they warm up to you, you might notice their legs uncross, and other barriers disappear. They might move a bit closer to you.

3. The might begin to gesture more and show you their palms.

4. They uncross their arms.

5. They might point or lean their body toward you.

Taking the initiative could help others open up to you. We all unconsciously start to copy the body language of other people. You can reverse this process by getting into a defensive posture.

The speed of the process all depends on the culture, character whether or not they are extrovert or introvert, and context like meeting a stranger on the street versus meeting them at a party.

Universal Non-Verbal Signals

Non-verbal communication will be different for everyone, and it is in different cultures.

A person's cultural background will define their non-verbal communication because some types of communication, such as signals and signs, have to be learned.

Because there are various meanings in non-verbal communication, there can be miscommunication could happen when people of different cultures communicate. People might offend another person without actually meaning to because of the cultural differences. Facial expressions are very similar around the world.

There are seven micro-expressions that are universal, and we will go more in depth about these in a later chapter, but they are content/hate, surprise, anger, fear, disgust, sadness, and happiness.

It could also be different to the extent of how people show these feelings because, in certain cultures, people might openly show them where others don't.

You are an American, and you take a trip to Italy. You don't speak Italian. You don't take a translator with you, and you forgot your translation dictionary. You have to rely on non-verbal communication in order to communicate with others.

You found a nice quiet restaurant you want to try so you point at your selection on the menu. You pay your bill and leave. The workers nod at you as you leave being a satisfied customer.

There could be other times when things won't go as well due to non-verbal communication such as people not making eye contact or they get offended when you do make eye contact.

Nods could also have various meanings, and this causes problems.

Some cultures their people might not say "yes," but people from a different culture will interpret as "no." If you nod in Japan, they will interpret it as you are listening to them.

Here are different non-verbal communications and how they differ in various cultures:

- Physical Space

People in various cultures will have different tolerances for the space between people. People from the Middle East like to be close together when they talk to others. Other people could be afraid to be close to others while talking.

Americans and Europeans don't have as much acceptance about people entering what they consider their physical space. This is even less when talking about Asians. Everyone will have their own personal space that they don't want others to enter. There are many cultures where close contact between strangers is very acceptable.

- Paralanguage

The way we speak constitutes what we talk about. Pitch, rhythm, volume, vocal tones, can speak more than what the words are actually expressing. Asian people can keep themselves from shouting because they have been taught from childhood that this isn't acceptable.

This is what is known as vocal qualifiers. Yelling, whining, and crying are vocal characterizations that can change the message's meaning. In certain cultures, giggling is a very bad gesture. There are several emotions that can be expressed through vocal differences but are all a part of a person's paralanguage.

- Facial Expressions

Our faces can show emotions, attitudes, and feelings. Cultures can determine the degree of these expressions. Americans will show emotions more than people from Asia.

Most facial expressions are the same throughout the world, but certain cultures won't show them in public. These meanings are acknowledged everywhere. Showing too much expression can be taken as being shallow in certain places where others take it as being weak.

- Posture and Body Movement

People can get a message or information from the way your body moves. It can show how a person feels or thinks about you. If they don't face you when you are talking, it might mean that they are shy or nervous. It could also show that they really don't want to be talking with you. Other movements such as sitting far away or near someone could show that they are trying to control the environment. They might be trying to show power or confidence.

A person's posture such as sitting slouched or straight can show their mental condition. Having their hands in their pockets could show disrespect in various cultures. If you are in Turkey or Ghana, don't sit with your legs crossed as this is considered offensive.

- Appearance

This is another good form of non-verbal communication. People have always been judged for their appearance. Differences in clothing and racial differences can tell a lot about anyone.

Making yourself look good is an important personality trait in many cultures. What is thought to be good appearance will vary from culture to culture. How modest you get measured by your appearance.

- Touch

Touch can be considered rude in many cultures. Most cultures view shaking hands as acceptable. Hugs and kissing, along with other touches, are viewed differently in various cultures. Asians are very conservative with these types of communications.

Patting a person's shoulder or head has various meaning in different cultures, too. Patting a child's head in Asia is very bad because their head is a sacred piece of their body. Middle Eastern countries consider people of opposite genders touching as being very bad character traits. How and where a person is touched can change the meaning of the touch. You have to be careful if you travel to different places.

- Gestures

You have to be careful with a thumbs up because different cultures view it differently. Some could see it as meaning "okay" in some cultures but being vulgar in Latin America. Japan looks at is as money.

Snapping your fingers might be fine in some cultures but taken as offensive and disrespectful in others. In certain Middle Eastern countries, showing your feet is offensive. Pointing your finger is an insult in some cultures. People in Polynesia will stick out their tongue when they greet someone, but in most cultures, this is a sign of mockery.

- Eye Contact

Most Western cultures consider eye contact a good gesture. This shows honesty, confidence, and attentiveness. Cultures like Native American, Hispanic, Middle Eastern and Asian don't make eye contact as a good gesture. It is thought to be offensive and rude.

Unlike Western cultures that think it is respectful, others don't think this way. In Eastern countries, women absolutely can't make eye contact with men because it shows sexual interest or power. Most cultures accept gazes as just showing an expression but staring is thought to be rude in many.

Chapter 5

The Secret is in The Breath

There are various ways you can read a person's body language. You can read it by their arm and leg movements, facial expressions, smiles, or eye contact. But did you know that the way you breathe has meanings also?

Emotions and the way you breathe have connections. You can read a person's feeling by watching their breathing. If your emotions change, the way you breathe can be affected.

See if you can notice breathing patterns in your coworkers, family, friend, or partner.

They might not tell you exactly how the person is feeling, and it could depend on a specific situation.

- Sighing might be a signal of sadness, hopelessness, or relief

When you sigh, you let out a deep, long breath that has an audible sound. Someone might sigh if they feel relieved like after a struggle has passed. They are probably thankful that this struggle is over. A sigh could also show hopelessness or sadness, like someone waiting for their date to show up. It might also show disappointment and tiredness.

- Rapid, heavy breathing might show fear and tiredness

You might have just seen a person rob a place and they are being chased by the police. You notice they are both breathing very rapidly. This is because the lungs need more oxygen because they are exerting a lot of energy due to the running. Their bodies are feeling tired, and their lungs are trying to keep up. We will feel the same effects when we get scared. This happens because when we experience fear, our lungs need extra oxygen, so we start to breathe faster. You can easily see when someone has been scared or running by noticing how they are breathing.

- Deep breathing could indicate attraction, love, excitement, fear or anger

Breathing deeply is the easiest breathing patterns to spot. If someone suddenly begins to hold their breath, they might be feeling a bit scared. If a person takes a deep breath and then shouts, they might be angry. People, who feel excited, are surprised, or experience shock could suck in a deep breath. They can also take in a deep breath and hold it for a second or so. If their eyes begin to glow, this could indicate they are excited or surprised. A person might begin to breathe deeply if they are attracted to someone. You might notice someone take a deep breath in, suck in their stomach, and push out their chest in order to impress someone they are attracted to.

Conclusion

Thank for making it through to the end of this book, let's hope it was informative and able to provide you with all of the tools you need to achieve your goals whatever they may be. Being able to read people is a great skill to have in life. The uses of this skill are endless. Being a walking lie detector is an amazing ability, and a person will never be able to trick you again. Keep in mind that everybody is different. Aside from the universal signals, there may be some signs that are different for people. There are some people may pick at their nails when they are anxious, and others do it when they are upset. Make sure you get to know the person a little before assuming anything based on their movements.

Finally, if you found this book useful in any way, a review on Amazon is always appreciated!